TIPS FOR HAVING A MORE UNIQUE AND SPECIAL RELATIONSHIP WITH JESUS

1. get down on your knees and pray.

Here are 5 suggestions for developing your faith and deepening your connection with God.To pray is to do more than just say words. It's an opportunity to talk to the Creator directly. You can pray whenever you choose, but a good time to start is first thing in the morning. When you switch off your alarm and welcome the new day, remember to give thanks to God. Thank Him for the people in your life, the places you call home and the ways you go to work.

If you like what you're reading, please give us a like.

It's easy to lose sight of our good fortune in the hustle and bustle of daily life. You can keep these bright spots front and center by giving yourself time to think about them first thing in the morning and once more just before bed.

Pray that God would keep you and your loved ones safe. If you're having trouble keeping your mind on God's will, this is a terrific moment to beg for His assistance. Inquiring of God can often open our eyes to previously unseen possibilities.

MEDITATIVE NOTES

2. Get into the Bible and Dig In!

Consider the Bible a reference book. The pages have more wisdom on how to live than you might think. The letters to the churches (such as Ephesians and Philippians) and books like Proverbs provide instruction on how to conduct oneself as a Christian. The Bible is a treasure trove of wisdom.

The Gospels of Matthew, Mark, Luke, and John include Jesus' teachings, whereas the rest of the New Testament contains the teachings of Jesus' disciples. The Old Testament tells the stories of the forefathers of Jesus and other people of religion. The more you grow in God's Word, the less you'll let the world shake you.

To extract the most wisdom from the Bible, it is best to study one book in depth, whether in a classroom setting or independently. It will also become more obvious how this reality pertains to your situation.

MEDITATIVE NOTES

3. Associate with a Community of Believers

How to Develop Your Faith and Deepen Your Connection with GodAs a Christian, the fellowship is crucial to your development as a person and as a believer. You can find other Christians to talk to and share your opinions and experiences with at a local church, a Bible study in someone's home, or an internet forum.

It's possible to find Christian communities that gather around a common hobby or activity, depending on where you reside. Faith-based exercise courses, Christian literature clubs, and Christian counseling groups are all examples.

It's been said that you end up just like the five individuals you spend the most time with. Select Christian friends who are mature in their faith and can aid in your development as a follower of Christ.

MEDITATIVE NOTES

4. Serve Others

According to Jesus, "Therefore, whatever you want men to do to you, do also to them, for this is the Law and the Prophets" (Matthew 7:12, New King James Version).

Reciprocate with kindness and consideration. How frequently do we actually comply with this instruction after hearing it, though? How, therefore, does helping other people help you grow closer to God?

Jesus's life on Earth is our model for the kind of love and service to others that God desires from us. What happens if people harm and betray us? Yes. Even Jesus was hurt and betrayed by them. Even yet, he continued to reach out and direct people to God. When we provide for the needs of the needy, we are actually caring for Jesus' chosen. After asking Peter three times if he loved Him, Jesus finally responded, "Feed my sheep."

Graze my sheep. Our duty is to serve as the Lord's hands and feet, tending to the needs of others around us. To become closer to God, obedience is essential. Jesus stated, "If you love me, you will keep my commands." New International Version (John 14:15).

MEDITATIVE NOTES

5. Goodness, and faithfulness, have also been bestowed upon you. Your vocation may be the source of some of the gifts you receive. You can improve these abilities by engaging in specific actions. Your relationship with God can be strengthened by using the spiritual gifts God has given you to fulfill your life's mission and to serve others.

These are your innate qualities and abilities. Do you enjoy helping people, perhaps by making house calls or providing meals for them? Do you often find yourself in a teaching capacity? How often do you share the gospel with others?

Some other spiritual abilities you or others may possess are:

Consider the Bible a collection of letters and books written directly to you by God, and read them as such.[1] To learn about God, one must first hear what He has to say. One should read the Bible in order, beginning with Genesis and ending with Revelations. To learn more about Christ and how he made provision for your spiritual life, you could also begin with the Gospel of John. He completed the Salvation Plan so that all people, regardless of their past, may have a fresh start in Christ.

MEDITATIVE NOTES

6. Picture of the Christian ideal of developing a personal relationship with God. Third, prioritize God's will above everything else and love God. To love God with all your heart, all your soul, and all your mind is the greatest commandment in the law. Matthew 22:35-38. God's commands are not burdensome, and those who love God will follow them (1 John 5:3). By obeying His precepts, we can be sure that we know Him. Anyone who claims familiarity with God but doesn't obey his teachings is lying. But he who keeps his word is a man after God's own heart; such a man has demonstrated the fullness of God's love. One who claims to be His follower is expected to model his behavior after Christ's (1 John 2:6). Additionally, Jesus commanded, "If ye love me, keep my commandments" (John 14:15).

MEDITATIVE NOTES

7. Be kind and loving to one another.

Titled Image Develop your faith in God (the Christian God). Love your neighbor as you love yourself is Step 4. (Lev 19:18) Jesus called this the second greatest commandment, equal to the first, which is to love God; he claimed that all the other commandments hang from these two. In the Gospel of Matthew (Chapters 22:39-41) When we invest in our connections with people, we are also investing in our connection with God. One must love God with all their being.

Love God with all your heart, soul, and mind; this is the greatest and first commandment in the Law. If you truly want to become closer to God, you must give yourself over to Him.

When asked, "Teacher, what is the greatest commandment in the Law?" Moreover, he instructed him, "You shall love the Lord your God with all your heart, all your soul, and all your mind." This is the most important rule of all. Verse 36-38 of Matthew ESV

MEDITATIVE NOTES

8. Care for your community.

Truly, God has affection for His people. Therefore, if you wish to deepen your connection with God, focus on cultivating positive relationships with others around you. You can't get along with God if you're always picking fights with other people. Therefore, be kind to them, offer assistance, and keep the peace.

And a second that's very similar is this: "You shall love your neighbor as yourself." Verse 39 of Matthew ESV

Honor your mom and dad.

You've spent most of your life sharing a house with your parents, siblings, and maybe some cousins. How can you have a good relationship with God, whom you have never seen, if you can't even have a good relationship with individuals you've seen your whole life? Therefore, to improve your relationship with God, learn to love, honor, and respect your parents and siblings.

One who says they love God but hates their brother or sister is not telling the truth. To put it another way, 1 John 4:20 NIV states, "Whoever does not love their brother and sister, whom they have seen, cannot love God, whom they have not seen."

MEDITATIVE NOTES

9. Honor your partner.

The person you choose to spend the rest of your life with is your spouse or wife. God requires wives to respect their husbands and husbands to love their wives as themselves. Do not harm your spouse if you value your connection with God. Stay faithful to your wife. Keep your husband's honor intact. But let God be the focus of your marriage as you treasure your affection for one another and your children.

Yet let each of you love your own wife as himself, and let the woman show that she respects her husband. Ephesians 5:33 NKJV

Realize God.

You can't love God with all your heart if you don't know who He is.

Therefore, deepen your relationship with God by learning more about who He is. To get to know and understand God better, study His words and teachings in the Bible, hear about Him from a genuine preacher, and put what you've learned into practice in your daily life.

"Whoever does not love, does not know God, because God is love." NIV 1 John 4:8

MEDITATIVE NOTES

Made in the USA
Monee, IL
10 March 2024

54795632R00026